Tribute to Henry A. "Hank" Rosso

THIS WORKBOOK SERIES is dedicated to the legacy of Henry A. "Hank" Rosso, noted by many experts as one of the leading figures in the development of organized philanthropic fund raising in the twentieth century. This series of workbooks, ranging from *Making Your Case for Support* to *Building Your Endowment*, was the last project he undertook before his health failed him. The Indiana University Center on Philanthropy, of which he was a founder, is honored to have been asked to complete this project on Hank's behalf. My colleagues and I dedicate this series to his memory.

I am grateful to my colleague Tim Seiler for agreeing to serve as editor. Tim is director of The Fund Raising School, the national and international training program that Hank started in 1974. It is appropriate that this workbook series be tied directly to concepts and materials taught by The Fund Raising School.

By carefully studying the practitioners and scholars in fund raising who came before him, Hank was able to codify and teach principles and techniques for effective philanthropic fund raising. Scores of practitioners who applied his principles have been successful in diversifying their philanthropic fund raising and donor bases in sustaining their worthy causes. Hank was constantly concerned that those who might most need the information of The Fund Raising School might least be able to access it. He developed special courses for small organizations and edited *Achieving Excellence in Fund Raising* to get information into the hands of practitioners. This workbook series was for Hank another attempt to put the tools of effective philanthropic fund raising into the hands of practitioners who could not get to The Fund Raising School courses.

We hope you find this material useful to you in your work. One of Hank's favorite sayings was, "You can raise a lot more money with organized fund raising than you can with disorganized fund raising." We hope it helps you organize and find success in your fund raising activities. As you carry out your work, remember Hank's definition: "Fund raising is the gentle art of teaching the joy of giving."

Eugene R. Tempel
Executive Director
Indiana University Center on Philanthropy

FORTHCOMING BOOKS IN THE EXCELLENCE IN FUND RAISING WORKBOOK SERIES:

Developing Your Case for Support

Planning and Managing a Major Gifts Program

Setting Up Your Annual Fund

Building Your Endowment

EXCELLENCE IN FUND RAISING WORKBOOK SERIES TITLES AVAILABLE NOW:

Preparing Your Capital Campaign

Planning Special Events

THE JOSSEY-BASS NONPROFIT AND PUBLIC MANAGEMENT SERIES ALSO INCLUDES:

The Five Strategies for Fundraising Success, Mal Warwick

Conducting a Successful Capital Campaign, Second Edition, Kent E. Dove

Winning Grants Step by Step, Mim Carlson

The Fundraising Planner: A Working Model for Raising the Dollars You Need, Terry and Doug Schaff

The Jossey-Bass Guide to Strategic Communications for Nonprofits, Kathleen Bonk, Henry Griggs, Emily Tynes

Marketing Nonprofit Programs and Services, Douglas B. Herron

Transforming Fundraising: A Practical Guide to Evaluating and Strengthening Fundraising to Grow with Change, Judith E. Nichols

Achieving Excellence in Fund Raising, Henry A. Rosso and Associates

The Grantwriter's Start-Up Kit, Successful Images, Inc.

Secrets of Successful Grantsmanship, Susan L. Golden

The Excellence in Fund Raising Workbook Series

EXCELLENCE IN FUND RAISING

WORKBOOK SERIES

THE FUND RAISING WORKBOOK SERIES began with Hank Rosso and his vision of a set of separate yet interrelated workbooks designed to offer practical, high-quality models for successful fund raising. Each workbook focuses on a single topic and provides narrative material explaining the topic, worksheets, sample materials, and other practical advice. Designed and written for fund raising professionals, nonprofit leaders, and volunteers, the workbooks provide models and strategies for carrying out successful fund raising programs. The texts are based on the accumulated experience and wisdom of veteran fund raising professionals as validated by research, theory, and practice. Each workbook stands alone yet is part of a bigger whole. The workbooks are similar in format and design and use as their primary textual content the curriculum of The Fund Raising School as originally developed and written by Hank Rosso, Joe Mixer, and Lyle Cook. Hank selected or suggested authors for the series and intended to be coeditor of the series. The authors stay true to Hank's philosophy of fund raising, and the series is developed as a form of stewardship to Hank's ideals of ethical fund raising. All authors address how their contributions to the series act in tandem with the other steps in Hank's revolutionary Fund Raising Cycle, as illustrated here. It is the intent of the editor and of the publisher that this will be the premier hands-on workbook series for fund raisers and their volunteers.

Dedicated to the advancement of ethical fund raising

The Fund Raising School

Timothy L. Seiler

General Series Editor

Director, The Fund Raising School

Indiana University Center on Philanthropy

The Fund Raising Cycle

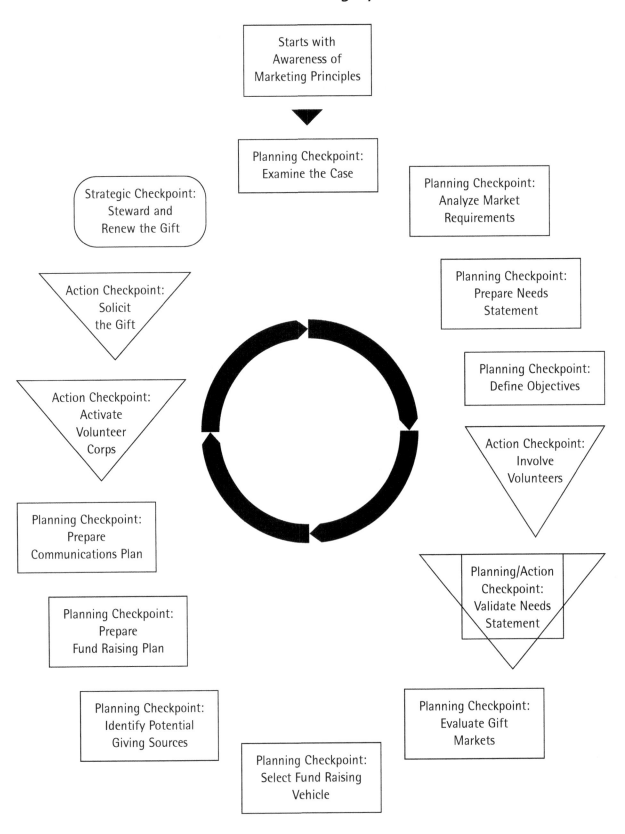

Starts with Awareness of Marketing Principles

Planning Checkpoint: Examine the Case

Planning Checkpoint: Analyze Market Requirements

Planning Checkpoint: Prepare Needs Statement

Planning Checkpoint: Define Objectives

Action Checkpoint: Involve Volunteers

Planning/Action Checkpoint: Validate Needs Statement

Planning Checkpoint: Evaluate Gift Markets

Planning Checkpoint: Select Fund Raising Vehicle

Planning Checkpoint: Identify Potential Giving Sources

Planning Checkpoint: Prepare Fund Raising Plan

Planning Checkpoint: Prepare Communications Plan

Action Checkpoint: Activate Volunteer Corps

Action Checkpoint: Solicit the Gift

Strategic Checkpoint: Steward and Renew the Gift

Source: Henry A. Rosso and Associates, *Achieving Excellence in Fund Raising*, p. 10. Copyright © 1991 Jossey-Bass Inc., Publishers. Reprinted by permission of Jossey-Bass Inc., a subsidiary of John Wiley & Sons, Inc.

BUILDING YOUR DIRECT MAIL PROGRAM

EXCELLENCE IN
FUND RAISING

WORKBOOK SERIES

Series Editor
Timothy L. Seiler

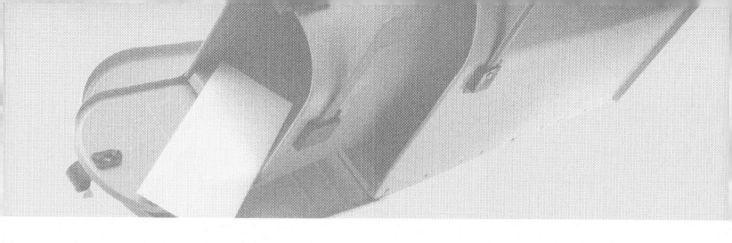

BUILDING YOUR DIRECT MAIL PROGRAM

GWYNETH J. LISTER, CFRE

JOSSEY-BASS
A Wiley Company
San Francisco

Library of Congress Cataloging-in-Publication Data

Lister, Gwyneth J.
   Building your direct mail program / Gwyneth J. Lister.—1st
ed.
          p. cm.—(The Jossey-Bass nonprofit and public
management series)
Includes bibliographical references.
   ISBN 0-7879-5529-9 (alk. paper)
   1. Direct-mail fund raising. I. Title. II. Series.
   HG177 .L57 2001
   658.15'224—dc21

2001000639

PB Printing   10 9 8 7 6 5 4 3 2 1   FIRST EDITION

The Jossey-Bass
Nonprofit and Public Management Series

This book is dedicated to Nina Brandt,
my first employer and friend in the nonprofit world.
Thank you, Nina, for teaching me
how important each donor is to the organization
and how to raise friends and funds.

Contents

Worksheets and Exhibits

Worksheets

Exhibits

Preface

THIS WORKBOOK is targeted to small and medium-size nonprofit organizations with no development staff or a very limited staff. The book is a step-by-step guide to the process of developing the direct mail component of a fund raising campaign.

What Is Direct Mail?

Direct mail refers to mailings of various types sent to present donors and to potential new donors (known as acquisition, cold, or prospect mailings) or others you might wish to contact through the mail. I use the terms *fund raising* and *fund development* interchangeably throughout the book; other terms associated with the direct mail process can be found at the end of Chapter One.

Using the Worksheets

Several chapters are followed by a worksheet that will help you analyze your situation and guide you in putting your direct mail package together. Each worksheet is important; none can be skipped. The worksheets will help you articulate, for example, why you are in business, why and how donors have supported your organization in the past, what makes a mail-friendly package successful, how to budget for your mailings, and how to evaluate each mailing. All of these components of your operation must be clear *to you* if you are to expect maximum return on your direct mail effort. Several worksheets are completed as samples; these will show you how to fill in the blank worksheets that accompany them.

The Importance of Mailings

Why would I write an entire book about mailings? I did it because I think readers should understand how important mailings can be; sometimes they produce critical support for your organization. Ongoing mailings to your supporters and to those you would like to include in your donor base will help give you a steady income over the years.

You know, of course, how pervasive direct mail is. It arrives in your mailbox every working day. Profit and nonprofit businesses and organizations send you information through the mail—information that has, in fact, produced results. You and many others have sent those organizations money. In fact, studies have shown that the reason most frequently given for making a gift to a nonprofit is, "I was asked to give." The use of the mail gives your organization an opportunity to ask for support, to explain what you are doing with donors' funds, and to keep in touch with donors. It also gives you the opportunity to find new supporters who are interested in the work you are doing.

Where Should Direct Mail Go?

Most direct mail goes to individuals. According to the AAFRC Trust for Philanthropy (Kaplan, 2000), total philanthropic giving in 1999 totaled $190.16 billion; 75.6 percent of these funds came from individuals who are living, and 8.2 percent came in the form of bequests. Thus fully 83.8 percent of the $190.16 billion came from individuals. Foundations accounted for 10.4 percent and corporations for 5.8 percent of the total donations.

Successful organizations try to reach everyone who is interested in their work—those who may have linkage with the organization (know the board members or staff members, for example) and those with the ability to donate funds. You can find these people by using direct mail; this workbook will show you how. You will learn the steps you must take to reach individuals who have the interest and the ability to give financial support to your organization, as well as to the many other important groups who are addressing the needs of society.

Planning Your Mailing

You are already an expert when it comes to direct mail because you have received hundreds of pieces of it from nonprofit organizations. But did you read them? Was their message of interest to you? Did they touch your heart?

Did you send money? If you have not been reading your mail from non-profit organizations, now is the time to start.

Mailing to your old supporters and new ones you hope to acquire can be exciting and rewarding if you (1) plan your mailings and (2) follow a few simple rules. I'll get to those. But first, ask yourself these questions as you begin to plan:

To whom should I mail?

What should my mail package look like, and when should it be sent?

What will be the return on my investment in direct mail?

How long should the letter be, and what should I include with the letter?

How do I say thank you?

How do I keep track of my direct mail donors?

This workbook will answer these questions and address other concerns you may have regarding the use of direct mail.

Other questions might include "Why don't I just raise money on the Internet?" or "Should I have a Web page?" Someday all funds may be raised on the Internet, but we're not there yet. A Web page is fine if you have a page that educates your donors and would-be donors. But doing that is a lot like sending a letter full of information regarding your programs and neglecting to ask for support in the way of a donation. Another drawback is that if your most likely donors are mature adults (over age sixty), you may have to wait awhile for them to get on-line. I understand that many well-known national organizations are receiving donations through the Internet. But you be the judge. Are you a large, national, well-known organization? If not, you are probably better off promoting your organization through the mail. You can both educate donors *and* ask for their support.

Steps Toward Developing a Successful Plan

I have based the steps in this book on the Fund Raising Cycle (see the illustration at the front of this book), first described by Hank Rosso in *Achieving Excellence in Fund Raising* (1991c). Rosso states that any fund raising effort must begin by knowing your market. Know who your customers are and what they want and need. In the nonprofit world, our markets include donors and volunteers, boards of directors, investors from foundations, and our staffs. One purpose of this book is to help you understand your donors and others who might make an investment in your organization.

Then you must be sure you understand why you're asking for donations. This seems to go without saying. You're asking for donations because you need money to continue what you're doing. But that's not a good enough case for support.

Understand Your Case

Why would someone invest in your organization? Ask yourself what would motivate recipients of your letter to make an investment in your organization and the work you do. Then give yourself plenty of time to plan your package.

Next, examine your case for existence. Why is your organization in business? Whom do you serve? Organizations can justify their existence only if they base their programs on valid needs. If the market lacks knowledge of the needs and the case of the organization and "deems the needs to be insignificant, then the possibilities for effective fund raising become negligible" (Rosso, 1991c, p. 11). Therefore, you must prepare a needs statement.

Prepare a Needs Statement

A needs statement is an analysis of your internal and external needs necessary to prepare your case statement. This will be discussed in detail in Chapter Two.

Review Your Donor List

Review your present donor files to find out who has supported your organization in the past. If you do not have a donor list, you will learn in this book how to build your own list of supporters. The package you send—the outer envelope, the letter, enclosures—will be discussed. You will learn what should be in the package and what should not be. Ideas for writing the letter, tracking your donations, and saying the big thank-you will be covered. An overview of postal rules and regulations and information regarding working with list brokers and mailing houses or a lettershop are included in the Resources section.

Outline Your Goals

The next step is to address your goals and objectives. The goals should be broad, such as "finding housing for all the homeless people in the local community." The objectives are more specific. They define, for example, how many people and how many housing units are needed to fulfill the goals. The objective must be a specific explanation of how the organization will achieve its goals.

Recruit Volunteers

Next, involve your volunteers. In the nonprofit sector, volunteers are the lifeblood of the organization. The staff cannot do the job alone. After you have involved volunteers, revisit the needs statement; volunteers can then be involved in a needs-validation process, thus giving the volunteers a strong sense of ownership and belonging.

Evaluate Gift Markets

The next checkpoint is to evaluate gift markets. Which gift sources might you approach? How much money is in the budget to be used for fund raising? Should you approach individuals, foundations, corporations, associations, or government agencies?

Select Fund Raising Vehicles

It is now time to select the fund raising vehicles you want to use. If your organization has a history of fund raising, review it for success or failure in producing funds. You may select direct mail, phone-a-thons, special events, gift clubs, capital campaigns, a major gift campaign, or planned giving. You should use as many of the vehicles as possible in order to reach all segments of your donor market, including, if appropriate, the direct mail that you are learning about in this book.

Identify Gift Sources

Then you want to identify gift sources. Research who you think should receive your mailings and then prepare a fund raising plan and a communications plan. Now the Fund Raising Cycle is in motion. Involve the volunteers, solicit the gifts, renew the gift, and start all over again. Evaluation of these steps should be taken every year as you complete one year and plan for the next. Annual planning must be ongoing. Four months before the start of your calendar or fiscal year, you should start planning for the coming year. How will you raise the funds needed for your organization to carry on its work? This planning should include all the strategies used in fund development, such as person-to-person solicitation of major gifts, special events, proposals to foundations and corporations, and mailings to individuals.

Individual support should be the backbone of your fund raising campaign—individuals, one at a time, who will support the organization year after year. You may, depending on your organization, include businesses, civic organizations, churches, and others in your direct mail plan.

Remember that people want to help make possible programs that they cannot carry out themselves but would like to see carried out. How do we find these people, make friends of them, and keep them as loyal donors? We do it one step at a time, as outlined in this workbook. So please take every step, and build your loyal donor base. Direct mail is very personal. It is a one-on-one relationship—a relationship that must be developed, nurtured, and maintained.

Does Direct Mail Work?

You may be thinking that this is all very interesting, but does direct mail work? Isn't there so much mailing coming at everybody these days that our own messages will be lost? Not necessarily. Researchers at the Indiana University Center on Philanthropy have created a new way of measuring how effective charities are at soliciting donations. The Philanthropic Giving Index (PGI) offers scientific measurement on current activities and predicts future trends based on fresh data. Findings in the first index (Keirouz and Rooney, 1998) include this statement: "The most popular fund raising techniques are the use of major gifts, followed by direct mail and planned giving." They also found that "planned giving and major gifts are especially successful techniques for organizations with more than $50 million in annual revenue." For the millions of organizations with annual revenue of less than $50 million, direct mail is the strategy of choice when contacting present supporters and acquiring new donors.

Of course, part of your yearly planning should also include the organized solicitation of major gifts and planned gifts, as well as contacts with foundations and corporations. But individual giving is the key to your fund raising success. Each year *Giving USA*, published by the AAFRC Trust for Philanthropy, reports on the sources of contributions. Overall and on average, individuals give about 82 to 85 percent of the funds received by nonprofit organizations. This includes outright donations, bequests, and planned gifts. With this figure in mind, it becomes clear that reaching out to individuals to support your cause is imperative and should be ongoing. A very effective and exciting way to reach individuals is through the mail. Through the mail you build a constituency loyal to your organization, educate the public regarding your cause, and find the funds to carry on your work.

You have a learning opportunity every day in your own mailbox. It is important to read and study every letter you receive from a nonprofit organization. Ask yourself what appeals to you and what would appeal to your constituency.

To be successful fund raisers, we must understand our markets, who our customers are, and what they want and need. The purpose of this book is to help you use direct mail to accomplish those goals.

Acknowledgments

First of all, I thank Henry A. Rosso for asking me to write this book. I have tried to write it with the enthusiasm for fund raising by mail that you always exhibited and taught to everyone who attended The Fund Raising School.

I thank all of my friends, children, and grandchildren, who kept asking if the book was finished yet. You really do keep a person on track.

I thank Skip Henderson, CFRE, and Alan Wendroff, CFRE, for your encouragement, good ideas, and support.

I thank Ann Cameron for your support and Carol Cameron for your proofreading efforts.

I thank the staff at Jossey-Bass and all who were kind enough to read the first draft of the book.

I thank Harry Schriebman, the computer wizard of Corte Madera.

I thank all of the wonderful people I have worked with in the field of philanthropy for your encouragement, dedication, and dreams.

Corte Madera, California   Gwyneth J. Lister
February 2001

The Author

GWYNETH J. LISTER has worked in the nonprofit field for more than twenty-five years as a development director or an executive director; since 1987 she has served as director of Accelerated Income Methods (AIM). As director of AIM she has worked with all types of nonprofit organizations in areas of fund development and management.

Lister started her career when she completed nurse's training at St. Mary's Hospital in San Francisco. After several years in the field of nursing, she entered the nonprofit field, taking a position in program development with the American Cancer Society. While working, she completed her undergraduate degree at Dominican College in business and psychology; she then completed her M.B.A. degree at Golden Gate University.

In 1994, Lister received the Outstanding Fund Raising Executive award from the Association of Fundraising Professionals (AFP), Golden Gate Chapter.

Lister is an adjunct faculty member of the University of San Francisco, College of Professional Studies. She has conducted classes for both the development directors' certificate program and the master's program. She is an adjunct faculty member of The Fund Raising School, Indiana University Center on Philanthropy. She teaches both the five-day course, "Principles and Techniques of Fund Raising" and the three-day course, "Fund Raising for the Small Shop."

Lister offers a wide variety of consulting services and has been a presenter at the Support Center in San Francisco, the Peninsula Community Foundation in San Mateo, the Foundation Center in San Francisco, and national and international conferences. She is a past board member of the AFP, both the national association and the Golden Gate Chapter. She is also a past president of the Development Executives Roundtable, San Francisco.

BUILDING YOUR DIRECT MAIL PROGRAM

Understanding Direct Mail Fund Raising

THIS CHAPTER will help you understand the importance and benefits of using the mail to keep in contact with donors and to ask for their support. It also highlights some basic steps one must take to raise funds—and friends—through the mail.

Direct mail can be the most exciting and rewarding way to keep in touch with your present donors and to reach new ones. Direct mail brings your organization to the doorstep and into the mailbox of the people who may be interested in your cause. If you learn how to use the mail effectively, you can reap exceptional benefits, find new friends for your organization, educate them, and build for the future of your cause.

But no organization is in a position to waste precious funds on direct mail if it will not bring a reasonable return to the organization. Once that piece of mail has left the office or mailing house, the organization has no control over what happens to it. Therefore, a great deal of time and thought must be invested in the preparation of the mail piece: who that piece is intended for, and how and when they will receive it. Will it touch the heart, catch the eye, and be opened? As Henry Rosso often said, "Touch the heart and ask the brain to send a gift."

But if the people you reach do open the mail you send them, will they take the action you suggest—to send a donation to support your very important work? One way to ensure that recipients will respond positively is to approach them in a positive way. For example, "With your support we will be able to shelter twenty additional families during this cold winter." In other words, let potential donors see a place for their donation in the work you are doing. I'll discuss this issue in more detail in Chapter Five.

Why Mail to Individuals?

In the Preface, I mentioned the value of mailing to individuals. Over the years, 82 to nearly 86 percent of the funds raised for philanthropy have come from individuals; in 1999, individual giving accounted for 83.8 percent of the total of $190.16 billion in donations (Kaplan, 2000). Roger M. Craver states, "By the estimates of some practicing specialists, direct mail is the medium that accounts for between $20 billion and $25 billion of the charitable educational and social change dollars contributed by Americans each year" (1991, p. 65). He also states, "The organization that asserts itself in learning the real purpose and proper use of this medium will reap significant rewards, discover new special-gift and major-gift prospects, educate its constituency, and reach its peripheral constituencies, thus making them more active contributors" (p. 65).

Individuals can learn about and support your organization through personal interaction. This strategy is used when we are asking the donor, face to face, for a special gift or a planned gift. It is a time-consuming activity and in most cases is used only to solicit large gifts. However, direct mail can be used to build your donor list so that individuals will become loyal—and possibly large—donors in the future.

The telephone can also be used to contact would-be donors or a committed constituency such as alumni. However, cold calling, calling someone you do not know or have not had contact with, is not usually a cost-effective way to raise funds. The donor list must be built. You can do this by looking for people who have an interest in your cause or have some link with your board of directors, your volunteers, or your staff. And of course, you should look for people who are in a position to make a donation to your organization.

Mail is a cost-effective way to raise funds and friends if you use it carefully. Mail makes it possible to reach the largest number of individuals, to let them know the need your organization addresses, and to ask for their investment in your cause. Other means of communication can tell the story of your cause—newspapers, radio, and television—but these media outlets do not give donors a quick and easy reply form they can use to give their support.

The experience of many fund raising professionals has shown that most nonprofit organizations lose 25 to 30 percent of their donors each year. Donors leave for reasons beyond anyone's control. The mail is a vehicle that keeps you in touch with your present donors and gives you the opportunity to acquire new ones. Direct mail builds a foundation or base of donors—it is most effective in bringing in a new gift, renewing gifts, and upgrading gifts.

Types of Direct Mailings

There are two types of mailings: (1) house list mailings (to people who have supported the organization in the past) and (2) acquisition mailings (to potential new donors). The latter type are also known as cold list or prospect mailings. Whichever type of mailing you plan to do, you must consider several questions:

- Why are we doing this mailing, and who are we trying to reach? What are the needs of our audience? What benefits will they derive from responding to this solicitation?

- How much will this mailing cost, and what can we expect in return?

- What will be the theme of this mailing? Do we have a story to tell that will engage the donor, or a problem that the donor might be interested in helping us solve?

- When should the package arrive in the hands of the would-be donor?

- Have we enclosed in the package a handy response form? Is it a clean package—one not cluttered with extraneous materials?

- Is the message clear and to the point?

Every mailing must be evaluated. This is done by keeping track of all mailings—when they were sent, the number mailed, what was in the mailing, and how the returns can be tracked. Mailings must have a code on the return piece or the return envelope. This process will be discussed in detail in Chapter Eight.

Timeline for a Mailing

If you are wondering how long it takes to put a mailing together and get it in the mail, here's a typical timeline. First, select the type of mailing (house list, prospect mailing, or special mailing) you want to do. The timeline for most mailings might look like this one for a house list mailing:

Task	Time Before Mail Date
Start copy and design work	12 weeks
Get copy and design approved	9 weeks
Send final letter, enclosures, and reply to printer	7 weeks
Check and approve blueline at printers	6 weeks
Have package at the mailing house	2 weeks

There are variations, of course. If you are running the address labels yourself and volunteers are getting your mailing ready for the post office, you will have to make adjustments in the timeline. If this is a prospect mailing and you need to order mailing lists and work with a list broker, you should add at least four weeks.

The important thing is to make a timeline and give yourself an extra week or so for those unexpected challenges that always seem to pop up. As soon as this mailing is at the post office, start working on the next letter and mailing.

When do you count results? On an average, you can start counting your results in about six weeks and should have the bulk of your donations in three months.

Terms Used in Direct Mailing

Here are some terms used in direct mailing that you might not be familiar with.

Acquisition mailing: a mailing to persons who are not donors but are prospects for the purpose of acquiring new donors or members. These mailings are often called *prospect mailings.*

Annual fund development plan: an overall plan for fund raising that usually includes proposals to foundations and corporations, special events, a mailing plan, major gift solicitation, and phone-a-thons. This is a twelve- to eighteen-month plan.

Blueline: final proof before printing. The proof will closely resemble your final product, so you must examine it carefully.

Bulk mail: a third-class mailing of at least two hundred identical pieces per mailing. Nonprofit organizations pay a yearly fee for their bulk mail permit and are allowed to mail at a discounted rate (see Resources).

Business reply envelope (BRE, also called a wallet-flap reply envelope): an envelope that is preaddressed to the nonprofit organization. This envelope may outline ways to give a donation and has an opening for the donor's check or cash.

House list: list of names, addresses, and telephone numbers of donors compiled by the organization.

Indicia: a preprinted marking on each piece of bulk mailing that shows payment of postage by the sender. An indicia contains the organization's name and bulk mailing permit number; it may be used in place of a postage stamp or metered stamp.

Insert: any item, such as a brochure or pamphlet, that is placed in a direct mail package.

Layout: arrangement of text blocks, headlines, and graphics on a page.

Lettershop: a company that personalizes, labels, sorts, and stuffs envelopes in preparation for bulk mailings. A company like this is also referred to as a *mailing house.*

List broker: an individual or company that brings together owners of lists and direct mailers who use them.

List compiler: an individual or company that specializes in gathering names, addresses, and information from various sources to produce a customized list of prospective donors.

Merge-purge: process of combining two or more mailing lists into a single list and deleting duplicate names and addresses.

Nonprofit stamps: These stamps are a marketing tool for mailers who believe that donors will more readily open mail with a stamp than metered or indicia mail.

Sorting: arrangement of pieces in a bulk mailing by ZIP code to facilitate processing and more reliable delivery.

Tracking: maintaining records concerning various aspects of mailings such as response rate, date mailed, and location of respondents.

White space: areas on a page that have no printing on them.

Window envelopes: envelopes that have an opening through which an address printed on an insert is visible.

Your printer or list broker may also use special terms. Some printers will give you a booklet that explains the printing process and the terms used. If yours doesn't and you don't understand the terms, ask for an explanation.

CHAPTER 2

Creating Your Case for Support

THIS CHAPTER will show you how to build your case for support. The case is created as an internal document that states why you are in business, what you plan to do or are doing, and how you hope to accomplish your goals. You will use the case as a basis on which to communicate with donors and would-be donors. In other words, you will use your case as a basis for your marketing efforts.

What Is a Case?

Your case description of why you are in business and what you are doing or will do should mesh with your marketing strategies, which I'll discuss later in the chapter. Your case is a document from which you draw information when writing a fund raising letter or a proposal to a foundation. It states your mission (why your organization is here), your goals (what you are going to do), and your objectives (how you plan to accomplish all of these wonderful things).

Contents of the Case Statement

Before building your case, you will have to spend some time analyzing the present state of the organization. Use the following case statement outline (provided courtesy of The Fund Raising School) to clarify your future needs. It will help you determine what must be changed or added as you build your case.

A case statement should include the following information. A sample case statement appears in Worksheet 2.1B at the end of this chapter.

1. Mission (Why do we exist?)

    A. Philosophical

    B. Human/societal need

    C. Values

2. Goals (What do we want to achieve?)

    Objectives (How will we achieve the goals)?

    Programs and services (Which methods will we use)?

    Governance

    Staffing

    Facilities or mechanics of service delivery

    Finances (narrative, numerical, graphic)

    Total expense and income

    Philanthropic support required

    Strategic planning and program evaluation

    History

The use of the case for support will depend on the size and age of each organization and what you intend to accomplish with a specific mailing. "People give to resolve problems, to capture opportunities, to serve a purpose much larger than themselves" (Rosso, 1991b, p. 43). We must remember that motivation for giving may change over the years. Individual responses to different types of requests for support will also change. Yet the case must reflect the mission, goals, and objectives of the organization.

The case should also include financial and updated program information. Bruce Campbell (1998) notes that donors are very interested in financial accountability. When asked, "What information would most motivate you to give?" about one-third (32 percent) chose "the services the organization performs." But almost as many (28 percent) picked "how the donations are spent." Several pieces of information commonly perceived by fund raisers as very important were ranked as less motivating than the financial data, including number of people served (18 percent), individual success stories (14 percent), and the mission of the organization (8 percent).

Using the Case in Marketing

You cannot have a successful direct mail program without a strong and understandable case. You must also reach the right segment of the population that has some interest in your cause, some linkage with like organizations or people associated with your organization, and the ability and inclination to give funds for the support of your cause.

A LITTLE NEGLECT

A little neglect may breed great mischief. Indeed, Benjamin Franklin once said:

> For the want of a nail, the shoe was lost.
>
> For the want of a shoe, the horse was lost.
>
> And for the want of a horse, the rider was lost.

Please don't let the "want of a nail" lead to disaster for your organization.

Principles of Marketing

The principles of marketing suggest that two factors must be addressed before you start your mailing program: (1) your donors' *wants* and (2) your donors' *needs*. You must determine who might support you and what they will expect to receive in return for their support.

How do you go about learning the needs and the wants of your donors? People have *needs* but seek to fulfill their desires—their *wants*. For example, I may need a new car to get from point A to point B—just basic transportation. But I *want* all of the bells and whistles—the CD player, the sun roof. I will let my wants combine with my needs when I make the decision to purchase that new car.

As nonprofit organizations, we must know both the needs and wants of our supporters or potential supporters. We have to try to understand our donors. What do they want to receive in return for their support of your organization? Most small organizations do not have the time and money to do extensive market studies to find out what their donors want in return for their contribution. But these organizations can *ask* donors what is important to them and why they support the organization. These questions can be asked in informal conversations, through the use of a questionnaire, or in limited formal interviews. We can only inspire donors to give their support if we try to understand their needs and wants.

The Four P's of Marketing

Starting with a good case on which to build, next consider how to reach people to communicate that case to others outside your organization. That's where marketing comes in. Let's look at the four P's of marketing: *product, price, place,* and *promotion.* Each element will influence your mailing program.

Product

Is the product—your program—something donors are interested in supporting? Does it fill a need and want in their life? Can you explain why your program is important? Can you tell donors a story about, say, a thirty-five-year-old person who has just learned to read because of your program or the homeless family who has found housing and work because of your program? If you can explain your product—if you can bring it to life for others—you may find new and lasting supporters.

Price

What is the price for donors? Do they feel they are making a change in the lives of others? Did you ask them for the correct amount of money and thank them for their support—over and over again?

Place

When considering place in the mailing program, the question must be asked: "Did we make it easy for the donor to respond to our solicitation?" We do this by providing a return envelope that can be returned with as little effort as possible. We also do this by giving the donors an address and telephone number so they may contact us if they need information.

Promotion

Promotion refers, for example, to the addresses on your letters and the other materials in your presentation. Good promotion is based on the questions mentioned earlier: To whom are we sending this request for funds? How does our package look? Is it easy to read? Does it tell our story? Do we have a logo that people recognize? Have we made it easy to respond?

After you have written your case statement and begun to seriously consider how to market your cause, you are ready to begin organizing your direct mail program. If that program is to be successful, you'll need to be sure you know your own organization. That seems to go without saying, but it's not really so simple. If you are to project to the public your case for support, that case must be very clear in the minds of all who are part of the organization. Take the time to put your case together in written form. Keep it updated, in a binder or folder, so that you can refer to it when crafting a fund raising letter. Keep all of the letters sent over the years so that you can refer to them and know what you said in the past. And make sure everybody in your organization understands what you are doing.

It isn't easy to see what may motivate your donors. Past direct mail results may give you a clue. What type of solicitation has had the most positive response? The need to make such determinations explains why it is so important to keep accurate records of the response you have received from your past mailings.

Your case is a statement for future use when you are contacting donors or potential donors by mail. Once your case is in place—once you've written it and it's easy to find in a folder or a binder—you will be ready to use the case in external communications.

External communications include direct mail pieces, brochures, annual reports, and presentations to foundations and corporations.

COMMON MISTAKES IN A CASE STATEMENT

- The organization's reason for being is not well articulated. No vision is described, only goals.

- The problem or social need is unclear.

- The organization has failed to work with the board and staff to produce a clear mission or vision statement.

- The case statement is incomplete.

- The case statement is out of date and therefore not useful in today's market.

- The case statement is not kept in a central location (binder or folder) and referred to when needed, meaning that people must reinvent the wheel.

- The case statement is not reviewed annually.

Once again, keep in mind that most people cannot feed the hungry, shelter the homeless, provide medical care for those in need, build a university or hospital, or provide great music or art. They will, however, give you their support in order to accomplish these goals. Through the use of direct mail, you can find these people and ask for their investment.

Worksheets

Worksheet 2.1A will help you organize your mission, goals, and objectives as part of your case. Worksheet 2.1B has been completed to provide some guidance.

WORKSHEET 2.1A

Preparing Your Case

This worksheet will help you outline your readiness for direct mail fund raising. Fill it out using information about your organization. It will help you see how to articulate your case for support—the reasons donors should invest in your organization. You may wish to use the completed sample (Worksheet 2.1B) as a guide.

Name of Organization: _____

Mission: _____

1. Why is your organization in business? What societal need does your organization address? What is your mission?

2. What are your organization's goals for the coming year?

3. What are your organization's objectives for the coming year? In other words, how will you accomplish your goals?

WORKSHEET 2.1A (continued)

4. What programs or services do you offer?

5. What are your financial needs? Please break down your annual fund raising budget by strategies: mail, phone, personal solicitation, special events, foundations, corporations, and so forth.

6. Please add other elements of the case that are important to your cause and should be communicated to the public.

WORKSHEET 2.1B

Preparing Your Case (Sample)

You may use this worksheet as a guide for filling out Worksheet 2.1A.

Name of Organization: Mid-County Family Shelter

Mission: "No One Should Be Alone."

1. Why is your organization in business? What societal need does your organization address? What is your mission?

> The MCFS provides temporary and long-term shelter to women and their children, consulting, job training and placement, child care, and other services as needed. Temporary shelter is provided for three to four months; long-term shelter can be provided for up to one year. Help with transitional housing is provided. The organization serves twenty-two families at the present time. There is a need to serve at least ten additional families in the coming fiscal year.

2. What are your organization's goals for the coming year?

> We plan to raise funds to provide two additional long-term houses, serving five families each.
> We hope to increase the organization's staff by two persons in the field of fund raising.
> We plan to increase the board of directors membership by three persons from a present membership of seven.
> We hope to put together a board orientation packet and hold a board retreat and planning session.

3. What are your organization's objectives for the coming year? In other words, how will you accomplish your goals?

> We will provide the long-term housing by (1) working with the county regarding funds for homeless families, (2) increasing our fund raising ability by building our individual donors base, (3) contacting additional foundation and corporations.
> We have the funds to increase the fund development staff. In July we will advertise for these positions, interview candidates in August, and hire the new staff in September.
> Other plans are:
> To have in place an annual fund development plan by October 1
> To form an active governance committee by June 1
> To review candidates for the board positions and have new members on the board by August 1
> To hold a board retreat and planning session in early September.

WORKSHEET 2.1B (continued)

4. What programs or services do you offer?

In addition to the shelter, consulting, job training and job placement, and child care, we also work with the local schools to bring the children up to grade level and provide after-school tutoring. We work with the Country Health Department to provide medical and dental care for all of the family members.

5. What are your financial needs? Please break down your annual fund raising budget by strategies: mail, phone, personal solicitation, special events, foundations, corporations, and so forth.

Dates: 7/1/2001 to 6/30/2002	Estimate
Annual budget (fiscal year July 1, 2001, to June 30, 2002)	$300,000
Personal solicitation:	$50,000
Direct mail:	$75,000
Phone-a-thon:	0
Special events (net returns):	$25,000
Corporations:	$50,000
Foundations:	$75,000
Other: County funds:	$25,000

6. Please add other elements of the case that are important to your cause and should be communicated to the public.

We will need additional statistical information regarding the number of families needing our programs in the coming years.

CHAPTER 3

Identifying Your Donors

WHEN AN ORGANIZATION is starting to make its case and looking for funds to support its work, it contacts family, community, and corporate foundations. This is a good way to start, but it has limited potential. Foundations will provide support for a certain period of time—for example, they may contribute to your support for three years but will eventually start to ask how you plan to support yourself. Many times when they award your first grant, they ask how you intend to raise funds in the future.

Role of Special Events

A new organization often tries to raise funds through special events. Although special events are in most cases very labor-intensive, they have an important place in the fund raising mix. They not only bring in funding but also gain recognition for the organization in the community. And potential donors turn out for special events. It is important that you have the names and addresses of those who attend your special events so that you can contact them by mail afterward and ask for support. (For a discussion of how to assess your direct mail efforts, see Chapter Eight.)

New organizations often have a major donor who helps them get started. But will that donor be there year after year? What will happen when that donor decides that he or she has done enough for your organization? These considerations mean that you should start to build your individual donor base as soon as possible. I have seen many organizations depend on foundations, special events, or a major donor for several years but fail to bring donors into the organization and ask them for their ongoing support. Those organizations often ended up struggling financially.

Your donor base is made up of individuals who are interested in your work and have sent you support; they are your insurance for the future. Tell them—and using the mail is a big part of this effort—about the important work that is being done thanks to their support, and ask them once again to invest in the organization and the work it is doing.

Role of the Annual Fund

Henry Rosso (1991a, p. 52) outlines the primary objectives of an annual fund:

- To get the gift, to get it repeated, and to get it upgraded
- To build and develop a base of donors, and through this process to establish habits and patterns of giving
- To raise annual unrestricted and restricted money
- To use the donor base as a vital source of information to identify potential large donors
- To promote giving habits that encourage the contributor to make capital and planned gifts
- To remain fully accountable to the constituency through annual reports

You will need to analyze your present donor base, that is, find out who gives and how often donors respond to your solicitation appeals. The top 5 to 10 percent are your major donors at this time. Do you contact them in a special and personal way? If you have a donor base, it is time to segment it and decide how you will treat your large donors. Today, a large donor for your organization may give $500, but in five years a large donation may be $5,000—*if* you have built your donor base and treated your donors as your best friends.

An old Girl Scout song goes like this: "Make new friends and keep the old; one is silver, the other gold." The people on your present donor list are gold. Let them know they are very special to the organization. The new friends you will contact through the prospect or acquisition mailings are silver. Thank them and contact them often so they will become part of your gold team.

Worksheet 3.1A at the end of the chapter will help you analyze your present donor base. (If you do not have a present donor base, Chapter Four will instruct you how to find names for a donor base.)

Do you contact everyone following a special event and ask for support or give information regarding the work of your organization? What are the age of your donors, their average income, their special interests, and their links with your organization?

Where do they live, and what is their average gift? How do they give—by mail, at events? And what time of the year do you receive most of your income? Worksheet 3.1A is more than a tool to analyze your donor base and your donors' responses to your past mailings; you will also need it to determine the cost of your past mailings, the response rate, and the return on dollars invested.

If you don't know who your donors are and why they are interested in your organization, it may be time to conduct a market survey, do some formal and informal asking, or plan a focus group. Some sort of donor research should be ongoing and the results used in planning your strategies for annual giving.

Worksheets

You can use Worksheet 3.1A to help you identify donors in your own organization. The worksheet asks you to take a hard look at your present donor base (if you have one) and analyze the types of donors who support your cause. Why do they give? When do they give? What amount do they give? How do they give? Do they give memorial contributions? If so, will they give an outright contribution? Do they give at special events? Worksheet 3.1B is filled in as a sample that you may wish to consult for guidance.

WORKSHEET 3.1A

Analyzing Your Donor Base

This worksheet will demonstrate how data are used in the analysis of a donor base. If you do not have a donor list (or house file, as it is often called), proceed to Chapter Four to plan a prospect mailing. You may wish to use the completed sample (Worksheet 3.1B) as a guide.

Name of Organization: _____

1. How many active donors are in your house file? (Active donors are those who have given within the past eighteen months.)

   Active donors: _____

2. Segment this list according to giving levels:

   $1–$50   _____
   $51–$100   _____
   $101–$250   _____
   $251–$500   _____
   $501–$1,000   _____
   $1,001+   _____

3. List other categories you think are useful in this analysis:

4. What are the sources of your gifts? Were they received in response to a mailing? Which mailing?

   Mailing 1: Responses:
   Mailing 2: Responses:
   Mailing 3: Responses:
   Mailing 4: Responses:
   Newsletter responses:

   Other responses:

WORKSHEET 3.1A (continued)

5. For each of the categories in question 4, analyze the following: number of pieces mailed, number of responses, average gift, cost of the mailing, total income generated, net income, and cost to raise $1. (See example in Worksheet 3.1B: total income of $900 divided by total responses (45) = $20 as an average gift; $900 less the cost of the mailing, $315 = $585 in net income; expenses of $315 divided by contributions of $900 = 35 cents to raise $1).

Mailing 1:

Mailing 2:

Mailing 3:

Mailing 4:

Newsletter responses:

Other responses:

6. Donor demographics

Percentage of donors in _____ ZIP code: _____
Percentage of donors giving _____ times per year: _____
Any other demographic information you believe would be helpful in this analysis:

WORKSHEET 3.1B

Analyzing Your Donor Base (Sample)

You may use this worksheet as a guide for filling out Worksheet 3.1A.

Name of Organization: City Center

1. How many active donors are in your house file? (Active donors are those who have given within the past eighteen months.)

   Active donors   700

2. Segment this list according to giving levels:

$1–$50	600
$51–$100	50
$101–$250	30
$251–$500	20
$501–$1,000	0
$1,001+	0

3. List other categories you think are useful in this analysis:

   Gift-in-kind: IBM computer

4. What are the sources of your gifts? Were they received in response to a mailing? Which mailing?

Mailing 1: Responses:	45	House list	Short letter mentioning needs of clients
Mailing 2: Responses:	32	House list	Long letter about "what we have accomplished with your help"
Mailing 3: Responses:	56	House list	Letter from board telling how center helped one particular client
Mailing 4: Responses:	40	House list	Year-end letter including explanation of programs, annual report, and thank-you

   Newsletter responses: 5

   Other responses:

WORKSHEET 3.1B (continued)

5. For each of the categories in question 4, analyze the following: number of pieces mailed, number of responses, average gift, cost of the mailing, total income generated, net income, and cost to raise $1. (Example: total income of $900 divided by total responses (45) = $20 as an average gift; $900 less the cost of the mailing, $315 = $585 in net income; expenses of $315 divided by contributions of $900 = 35 cents to raise $1). Follow the example for Mailing 1 for each of the other mailings.

Mailing 1: Number mailed: 700   Number of responses: 45   Average gift: $20   Cost of mailing: $315
Total income: $900   Net income: $585   Cost to raise $1: 35 cents

Mailing 2: Number mailed: Number of responses: Average gift: Cost of mailing:
Total income: Net income: Cost to raise $1:

Mailing 3: Number mailed: Number of responses: Average gift: Cost of mailing:
Total income: Net income: Cost to raise $1:

Mailing 4: Number mailed: Number of responses: Average gift: Cost of mailing:
Total income: Net income: Cost to raise $1:

Newsletter: Number mailed: Number of responses: Average gift: Cost of mailing:
Total income: Net income: Cost to raise $1:

Other responses:

6. Donor demographics

Percentage of donors in 94925 ZIP code: 100 percent
Percentage of donors giving three times per year: 10 percent
Any other demographic information you believe would be helpful in this analysis:

In mailing 3, additional names from the board added fifteen new donors
30 percent of the mail-responsive donors live in the Highland Park area

CHAPTER 4

Building Your Donor Base

THIS CHAPTER and the worksheets that accompany it will help you create a base of donors and in the process find new friends and supporters. The ongoing loss of donors requires you to do a certain number of prospect or acquisition mailings each year.

I have asked many members of the public if they read the nonprofit mail they receive. Most say, "Oh, no, I don't read those letters." But several have added, "Unless it is a cause I am interested in." It is a fact of life that not everyone will be interested in your cause. Your job is to find out who may be interested and why.

Role of Prospect Mailing

How do you find out who's interested? One way to do it is to look at the donor lists from like organizations, buy lists, or trade lists, as well as ask people whether they are interested in the need you are addressing. To acquire this information, you can conduct a survey, do a test mailing, or hold face-to-face formal and informal interviews.

Prospect mailing will not bring the percentage return that your house list will produce. In some cases, a prospect or acquisition mailing may result in a financial loss for the first few years. If you mail again and again to those who have given from the prospect list, in a few years you will have made up the loss and added several new donors to your list of supporters.

At times it will be difficult to find information on would-be donors. Do they meet the profile of your present donors? Why would they be interested in the work you do? And what are you offering them in return for their support? Lists from members of the board of directors are quite powerful if the board members place a handwritten note on each letter and mention the organization when talking to their friends and business associates.

Role of Cold Mailing

A list of individuals who have *not* given to the organization before is referred to as a cold list. Some experts estimate you might expect a 1 to 2 percent return on such a mailing; others would say you should expect a financial loss. The returns on cold mailings may not cover the cost of the mailing, but the reason for these mailings is to acquire new donors who will give in the future—difficult though that idea might be to sell to your board of directors. However, you might point out that you lose donors each year; donors die, move away, or just lose interest in your cause. Cold mailings bring in new donors and give you the opportunity to make new friends for your organization.

If you ask these new donors at least four times per year, using a different approach each time you ask, you should make up the lost investment within three years. It will be necessary not only to compile these lists for cold mailings but also to test the list and the mailing package. Testing for a small mailing may not be possible, but ideas for testing will be discussed later in the book.

What to Do Before Any Mailing

Before you mail to your house list or any cold lists, certain essential business procedures must be in place:

- Having a system for keeping accurate records of all donors—names, addresses, phone numbers, and any other information you feel is important, such as linkage with board members, past volunteer activities, and so on

- Posting of the gift to the donor's records

- Having the ability to use source codes, that is, being able to identify why the gift was given (Was it in response to the May mailing or to a special event? Was it a memorial or in-honor-of gift?)

Fund raising software, discussed in Chapter Seven, is now available at a reasonable cost to help your organization keep track of this most important information. If you do not have it, you will be unable to evaluate the individual mailings. Many software packages give you the ability to send selected thank-you letters as you do your posting of gifts and to print out reports regarding mailing results. Most software packages come with specific built-in reports; thus the mailing results are at your fingertips with very little effort.

Role of Thank-You's

After any kind of mailing, the organization must have the ability to respond promptly to donations. Thank-you's must be sent within forty-eight hours of the time the gift was received. I discuss how to thank your donors in Chapter Nine.

Worksheets

Worksheet 4.1A will help you with prospecting—finding new donors and building your list. A filled-in version, Worksheet 4.1B, is provided as a sample.

WORKSHEET 4.1A

Building a Donor Base

This worksheet will guide you in your effort to build your organization's donor base. Worksheet 4.1B is filled out and may serve as a model.

Name of Organization: _____

1. When you are considering obtaining lists from members of the board of directors, think about the following:

   Number of board members: _____

   Number who would give you fifteen names and addresses and put a personal note on each letter: _____

   (Note: If you have ten board members and each is willing to give you fifteen names and put a personal note on each letter, you should be sending 150 letters. If the response is 10 percent, you should have fifteen new donors.)

   Number of new names and addresses from the board of directors: _____

   Number of new donors at a 10 percent response rate: _____

2. When you are planning ways to cultivate service club members, consider the following:

   A. Have you presented a program for the club? Does one of your board members belong to the club?

   B. List the clubs in your area that have some linkage with your organization:

   C. Who will ask these clubs for their membership list?

WORKSHEET 4.1A (continued)

3. What churches in your community might be interested in your work?

Who will ask these churches for the opportunity to mail to their members?

4. List other organizations or groups in your area who would allow you to mail to their members (consider sports clubs, college clubs, mothers' clubs, garden clubs, and so on).

Who should ask the group for the list?

5. Additional tips:

- Ask your staff, board members, and volunteers what groups they belong to and what groups might be interested in the work you are doing.

- Ask others outside your organization for suggestions about how to expand your donor list.

- Contact the County Health Department and the Office of Education for their support.

WORKSHEET 4.1B

Building a Donor Base (Sample)

You may use this worksheet as a guide for filling out Worksheet 4.1A.

Name of Organization: Stay Green Foundation

1. When you are considering obtaining lists from members of the board of directors, think about the following:

Number of board members: 10

Number who would give you fifteen names and addresses and put a personal note on each letter: 8

(Note: If you have ten board members and each is willing to give you fifteen names and put a personal note on each letter, you should be sending 150 letters. If the response is 10 percent, you should have fifteen new donors.)

Number of new names and addresses from the board of directors: 8 x 15 = 120

Number of new donors at a 10 percent response rate: 120 x .10 = 12

2. When you are planning ways to cultivate service club members, consider the following:

   A. Have you presented a program for the club? Does one of your board members belong to the club?

   Yes, I've presented a luncheon program for the Lions Club.

   B. List the clubs in your area that have some linkage with your organization:

   Lions Club: A board member belongs to this club and has an interest in homeless families.

   Highland Park Community Organization: A volunteer is with our organization.

   Downtown Professional Women: They are interested in issues facing women.

   C. Who will ask these clubs for their membership list?

   Board member will ask the Lion's Club.

   Mrs. Jones, a volunteer, will ask the Highland Park Community Organization for their list of members.

   The executive director belongs to the Downtown Professional Women and will speak at their next meeting.

3. What churches in your community might be interested in your work?

> Christian First Church, St. Patrick's Church

Who will ask these churches for the opportunity to mail to their members?

> Christian First Church: Executive director will ask for list.

> St. Patrick's Church: Mrs. O'Leary will ask for list.

4. List other organizations or groups in your area who would allow you to mail to their members (consider sports clubs, college clubs, mothers' clubs, garden clubs, and so on).

> PTA, Chamber of Commerce

Who should ask the group for the list?

> Secretary will approach.

5. Additional tips:

- Ask your staff, board members, and volunteers what groups they belong to and what groups might be interested in the work you are doing.

- Ask others outside your organization for suggestions about how to expand your donor list.

- Contact the County Health Department and the Office of Education for their support.

The Outer Envelope

The Letter

The Response Form

The Follow-Up Thank-You

Enclosures

CHAPTER 5

Assembling the Direct Mail Package

THE DIRECT MAIL PACKAGE can be used to reach out for volunteers, to inform the public of your activities, to invite people to special events, and for many other purposes. This chapter discusses the items that should be included in the direct mail package asking for support.

The direct mail fund raising package has several components, including the outer or carrier envelope, the letter, the response form, and an envelope (if needed) for the response form, along with any other items you plan to enclose. Of course, the mailing is based on having a good mailing list. We have discussed various lists and ways to build lists. Working with a list broker is discussed in the Resources section of this book.

The Outer Envelope

This, in most mailings, is a #10 envelope, measuring 4 by 10 inches. Your return address and logo should appear in the upper left-hand corner. Every time you use your logo, you are creating marketing awareness; people will start to recognize it and associate it with your organization.

In the upper right-hand corner you can place a first-class postage stamp. If you are mailing under your bulk mail permit (mailing at least two hundred identical pieces), you may use a nonprofit stamp, an indicia with your permit number, or metered postage. The Resources section describes U.S. Postal Service regulations for bulk mailing.

The address may be on a label or applied by a laser printer. Or the label could be affixed by the mailing house. The mailing house can offer you several types of labels, and you should decide which is best for your mailing. Of course, envelopes may be addressed by hand if the mailing is not too large and if you have the volunteer power for such a task.

"Change Service Requested" should be written or stamped on the outer envelope of all bulk mailings. This will cost you money when the undeliverable letters are returned to you (about 50 cents per piece), but eliminating these addresses will ensure that you will not be sending undeliverable letters in your next mailing. Furthermore, when envelopes are returned with a change of address, this lets you update your donor base with the new address and remail the letter to this new address.

There may also be a teaser on the outer envelope; the idea is to entice the supporter into opening the envelope. A teaser may be a picture of a child or an animal, or it may be a statement such as "You can help stop hunger, thirst, and disease in this desolate land."

TIPS FOR MAKING YOUR LETTERS EFFECTIVE

- Before you write your letter, get a clear picture of the person who will receive it.
- Involve the reader in the letter using the words *you* and *your, we* and *our.* Say, "You have made this happen" or "Our community is grateful for . . ."
- Use lots of white space.
- Use type that can be read by someone who wears glasses.

- Be sure the letter is delivered in a timely manner. A Thanksgiving letter that arrives on December 15 is a wasted opportunity.
- Ask for an investment in the work of the organization at least twice in the letter (once in the body of the letter and once in the postscript).
- Let the reader know that he or she is making a difference in the world or in the community. Be effusive with your thanks.

The Letter

In *Beyond Fund Raising,* Kay Sprinkel Grace (1997) states: "A simple formula for constructing a letter is (1) touch my heart, (2) tell me what the problem is, (3) tell me what you are doing about it, and (4) tell me how I can help" (p. 121). The letter should be long enough to tell your story and in type large enough to be read by someone who wears glasses. Ample white space should be left on the page. The letter may be constructed in the form of short bulletins, which give the reader an overview of your programs and accomplishments, or it may be a success story or a story of someone's struggle to overcome a grave problem.

The letter may be slanted to a certain holiday and have slogans such as "Open your heart on Valentine's Day," "Give a gift in memory on Memorial Day," or "We are thankful for your support at Thanksgiving." If the letter is three or four pages long, important entries should be underlined or printed in bold type.

When you are responsible for writing direct mail solicitation letters, you should first read all of the letters you have received from nonprofit organizations; these will help you decide what you like and what might appeal to your audience. When sending direct mail, it is very important to keep in mind the marketing principles I discussed in Chapter Two: What does the donor need and want? Do I need to send a different appeal to certain segments of the donor base, such as large donors, first-time donors, or donors who seem to respond to emotional solicitations versus factual solicitations?

The letter should be on official stationery and have a personalized salutation if possible. The personalized salutation is important when you are writing to your large or major donors.

The letter must also have a postscript (P.S.) as a call to action. Example: "P.S.: Your support today will provide holiday meals for many who would otherwise go hungry. In their name, we thank you." The P.S. is very important. Research has confirmed that the reader will read the P.S. first and then read the body of the letter.

Don't use long paragraphs or words. Write your letter to involve your reader, not to preach to your reader. Be sure to ask for financial support. Several helpful books on writing letters are listed in the Further Reading section at the end of this book. If you have not had experience writing letters of solicitation, these will be helpful. If you feel hopeless in this area, contact a direct mail consultant to start you off on the right track.

For-profit direct mail experts claim that letters account for 65 to 75 percent of all orders. Just sending a brochure will not bring the return that you may want or expect. Many organizations send an order form, but for-profit direct mail experts claim that an order form alone accounts for only 5 to 10 percent of orders received.

It is clear that the letter is very important, so after you have crafted it, have several persons who are not involved in the organization read it. Then craft it again. This is a difficult process, but when you write letters such as these, you must learn to remove your own ego and write to and for your audience.

A sample letter is presented in Exhibit 5.1. Be creative, be positive, and invite the reader to invest in the work your organization is doing. (If you cannot or do not want to use the person's name in the salutation, write "Dear Friend" or use a dramatic one-line opener, as in the letter in Exhibit 5.2.)

EXHIBIT 5.1

Sample Letter Asking for Support

January 18, 2001

Dear Mr. Evans:

On behalf of the Mid-County Family Shelter, I would like to thank you for your past support of our clients.

- During the past year, we have given emergency shelter to forty adults and sixteen children.
- Of those adults, thirty-eight were given housing in our shelter homes for sixteen to twenty-four months; twelve children were similarly sheltered.
- All of the adults have gone through our job training program; 70 percent have found work that will provide support for themselves and their children.
- All of the children have returned to school or are in our day-care program.
- Our counseling for the entire family is ongoing until families are stable and self-supporting.

Your past support has made all of this possible. We ask you once again to support these families who are working to put their lives back together.

Sincerely,
Donna Smith, Program Director

P.S. You have made a difference in the lives of others. Please continue your support. Thank you on behalf of the families you have helped.

A long letter (two to four pages) may be one of the four letters you send each year, or it may be a special letter to prospects who do not know the work of your organization. Include the following, in the order given, in a long letter:

Paragraph 1: an introduction to the work of the organization

Paragraph 2: an explanation of why this work is important to your community or the world

Paragraph 3: a story highlighting your accomplishments

Paragraph 4: the "ask" for support or an investment in your work

In this letter you bring the reader into the letter by using the word *you* and underlining or boldfacing words or paragraphs (see Exhibit 5.2). Whatever its length, the letter should be easy to read or scan. Say what is important and then stop. Let readers know they are making a difference in the world or in their community, and thank them sincerely and repeatedly.

EXHIBIT 5.2

Sample Dramatic Letter Asking for Support

December 1, 2000

We are powerless to help them without you!

Yesterday, Marie and her two children arrived at the shelter. They had been on the streets for several days, running from an abusive and out-of-control husband and father. A county worker brought them to the shelter, and of course we took them in and gave them food, a bath, and a clean bed.

The children, Lauren, age seven, and Mikey, age two, were very quiet and withdrawn—and Marie was fearful for her life and the lives of her children.

What will happen to Marie, Lauren, and Mikey?

We see women and children in this situation almost every day. With **your** help, we can help them put their lives back together again. We can arrange for counseling, financial support, job placement for Marie, school and child care for the children, and free legal and medical services—all things they desperately need to turn their lives around.

But we are powerless to help them without you! Please consider a tax-deductible gift to the Mid-County Family Shelter. We have enclosed a return envelope for your convenience. If you would like additional information regarding our programs, please call us at (555) 555-1234. On behalf of all our clients, we thank you for your concern for others and your support.

Sincerely,
Gerald Lang, Chairman, Board of Directors

P.S. Thank you for giving others the power to help themselves.

The Response Form

Several types of response forms can be sent to the donor. The response form both requests a response and provides ways to track each mailing. If you send me a letter without a response form, do you really think I am going to get an envelope, address it, and write out my check? Probably not. Make it easy for me to send you my contribution.

There are several different kinds of response forms. You may use a business reply envelope (BRE) like the one shown in Exhibits 5.3 and 5.4. This gives the donor several ways to support your organization. Donors may choose to make a memorial or in-honor-of gift, give through United Way, donate through company matching gifts, and so on. Give the donor as many ways as possible to support your cause.

EXHIBIT 5.3

Back and Front of a Business Reply Envelope

The Corte Madera Community Foundation has been established to encourage and receive contributions to be used in ways that will sustain and nurture the quality of life in Corte Madera.

Soaring Toward Community Enrichment

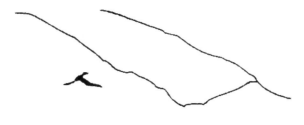

Corte Madera Community Foundation
Post Office Box 7109
Corte Madera CA 94976

EXHIBIT 5.4

Inside and Pocket of a Business Reply Envelope

Yes, I want to help keep Corte Madera a very special place in which to live. Enclosed is my check payable to the **Corte Madera Community Foundation.**
☐ **$35** ☐ **$50** ☐ **$100** ☐ **$250** ☐ Other $ _____

Name _____

Address _____

Town _____ Zip _____ Phone _____

☐ My employer has a Matching Gift Program and I will be asking my employer to match my donation. My employer is _____

☐ I would like to help Corte Madera by including the Foundation in my will. Please send me information.

☐ I would like to do volunteer work with the Corte Madera Community Foundation. Please contact me.

☐ I will use United Way's Donor Option Plan to make a gift to the Foundation.

- -

Please accept this donation:

In Memory of _____

In Honor of _____

☐ New Arrival ☐ Graduation ☐ Birthday ☐ Promotion ☐ Anniversary ☐ Other

Please send appropriate acknowledgment to:

Name _____

Address _____

City _____ State _____ Zip _____

Sign Card _____

(Contributions are tax deductible)
THANK YOU FOR YOUR SUPPORT OF OUR TOWN

Source: Both sides of business reply envelope from Corte Madera Community Foundation. Reprinted with permission.

If you use this form of response, you will need to code the envelope by marking each one so that you can evaluate your responses. A quick way to do this is to hold several envelopes in your hand and mark the sides with a colored marker; keep a list of the color codes you have used. For example, you may have marked your May mailing with a blue marker and your August mailing with a red marker. As the BREs are returned, you will need to enter the codes in your software system so that you can evaluate the returns from each mailing. It is very important to have a donor software system that allows you to enter the codes when you credit the amount given to the donor record. It is also important to have software that provides you with reports regarding who has given, the amount given, and which mailing the donor responded to. This is the only way to evaluate your direct mail efforts at the end of each quarter and year.

If you use a mailing house, the mailing house will code your mailings; the response form will have the donor's name and address, along with the code. Some forms give the donor a choice of options or the opportunity to join specific gift clubs. Other forms might include an opportunity to receive information regarding special gifts, such as gifts in wills or planned gifts. The response form is very important to your organization because you can track your returns to specific mailings and evaluate your efforts when the returns are complete.

If you use a BRE, you will not need a separate envelope for the reply form; all of the information should be on the BRE. Don't forget that the BRE must be coded. If you use a single reply form, you will need an envelope addressed to your organization.

Should you put postage on the reply envelope? Most direct mail experts say this is not necessary. Some organizations put a small note in the box at the right-hand corner of the envelope where the stamp will be attached. This note may say something like "Your stamp here will ensure that our services continue."

The Follow-Up Thank-You

Say thank you as many time as possible—in the letter, on the reply form, and after you have received the gift. Send that thank-you letter within forty-eight hours of receiving the gift. This is not fund raising; it is "friend raising."

The IRS requires specific wording in the thank-you note when the gift is over a certain amount of money or the donor has received something of value in exchange for a donation. Donors should be notified of what benefits to expect in return for a gift and the worth of those benefits. Information on the worth of benefits or premiums should appear on all fund raising literature and in the thank-you letters.

You should check with the IRS regarding the most recent rules that apply to receipts for donations. These rules change from time to time, and you are responsible for complying with them. Furthermore, IRS-approved wording must appear in the thank-you letter. For information regarding IRS regulations, call (877) 829-5500 or contact the INDEPENDENT SECTOR at (202) 467-6100. The IRS Web site is http://www.irs.gov.

Enclosures

Remember, too many enclosures may dilute the message that you are sending to your donors. I have always used this rule: *The more you enclose in the package, the less response you will receive.* If you enclose many additional pieces in the package, the reader may be confused or not even bother with your solicitation. We have all had the experience of many pieces of information coming out of the envelope. In a rush, we just dispose of the entire mess. So keep it simple and to the point: possible enclosures might be giveaway items (bookmark, key chain, address labels), a reprint from a news article, a reprint from an advertisement, or your own organization's brochure. Use items like these sparingly.

Many organizations include a BRE or a reply form in their newsletters. Such passive solicitations may raise enough to pay for postage on the newsletter but little else. You receive donations when you ask for donations. Most newsletters are informational or educational pieces. Include a BRE if you feel you must, but don't expect a large return.

CHAPTER 6

Planning Your Mailings

THIS CHAPTER shows you how to plan your direct mailings for a year. I think it's important to plan for at least a year to a year and a half. This gives you time to make adjustments if necessary.

If you're wondering why adjustments might be needed, consider these scenarios:

Some part of the plan you've made did not develop as you had hoped.

You did not receive that foundation grant.

Your major donor did not respond.

One of your mailings proved to be a great disappointment.

I believe that the annual plan for mailing should be reviewed at least every three months and adjusted. Remember that no plan is written in stone. In successful organizations, adjustments are made quickly as external and internal factors change.

How Often to Mail

I recommend mailing to your house list at least four times per year; do some acquisition mailings and mailings to segments of your present list, and send a special letter to large donors or donors who have given for a specific reason. Each of these mailings must be part of your annual plan to raise funds; each will need funds to get them from the drawing board into the hands of the donors.

Mailings can be expensive, and you need up-front funds in order to do them, but do not be discouraged if you do not have the funds to do all of the mailings in your plan. Take it one step at a time. It may work to have a mailing underwritten by a local business or corporation that would be happy to see a notation on the mailing that looks something like this: "This mailing was made possible by a grant from John's Hardware. One hundred percent of your donation will be used for the homeless in our community."

When to Do Special Mailings

The special mailings described in Worksheet 6.1 (at the end of the chapter) may include a mailing to lapsed donors. These are donors you have contacted four times per year who have not responded for at least two years. Send a very special letter inviting them to make an investment once again in the work of the organization. You may point out some of the positive things that the organization has done over the past two or three years.

One successful mailing I was involved with was a mailing to lapsed donors. It was the twenty-fifth anniversary of the organization, and all lapsed donors received a letter and a leather bookmark with the logo and the anniversary date. The response was a 50 percent return of lapsed donors. Be creative when addressing your lapsed donors, but keep track of these folks and invite them to invest once again.

These mailings are done to build your donor list. We do lose donors over the years. If you lose 25 percent of your donors each year and you have a donor list of 1,000 donors, in four years you will have no donors. Mailing to prospects may bring you some very special donors who will stay with you for years. You may not fit the average. These acquisition or cold mailings may bring donors that may stay with you for life, become major donors, and remember your organization with planned gifts or bequests. Of course, this means you must keep in touch with your newfound donors by mail, by phone, or in person.

In any case, it is important to take a good look at your donor list each year and make an estimate of the donors you are losing. I have found that some faith-based organization keep their donors for many years, whereas other organizations and donors go in and out of fashion.

Will donors become upset with the organization for sending so many solicitation requests? Probably not. But if they do express concern, be sure to honor their wishes and send them only one or two mailings per year. Know your donors and treat them as your best friends, which they are.

Chapter Seven will provide additional planning information; you will see how to assess your costs. With that, you should have enough information to plan your own budget.

Worksheets

Worksheet 6.1 outlines a one-year plan for direct mail. It also shows how to include a special mailing for a new or special program, upgrading of a facility, or raising funds to match a gift. For example, someone may offer you $5,000 if you can raise matching funds. For every dollar your donor gives, your organization will receive another dollar as a matching gift. In most cases, this mailing would be in addition to your four mailings per year. By completing the worksheet, you'll be better able to make decisions regarding the mailings to your house list.

Worksheet 6.2 specifically addresses your mailings to people you do not know but feel may have an interest in your cause. This worksheet includes your acquisition, prospect, or cold mailings.

After you have completed Worksheet 6.3 and have estimated your mailing costs, you should have enough information to build your own budget so you have the funds to accomplish these mailings. This worksheet will help you decide how to mail to your house list.

WORKSHEET 6.1

A One-Year Plan for Direct Mail

This plan outlines a direct mail program. I recommend that you plan for at least a year, preferably a year and a half.

Name of Organization: _____

Budget Dates: _____

This plan includes

_____ mailings to donors on the house list

_____ mailings to acquire new donors

_____ special mailings

House List Mailings

Event	Date
Mailing 1 begins	_____
All material goes to printer	_____
Envelopes stuffed and ready for post office	_____
Mailing delivered to post office	_____
Mailing 2 begins	_____
All material goes to printer	_____
Envelopes stuffed and ready for post office	_____
Mailing delivered to post office	_____
Mailing 3 begins	_____
All material goes to printer	_____
Envelopes stuffed and ready for post office	_____
Mailing delivered to post office	_____
Mailing 4 begins	_____
All material to printer	_____
Envelopes stuffed and ready for post office	_____
Mailing delivered to post office	_____
Total cost of house list mailings:	_____

WORKSHEET 6.1 (continued)

Acquisition Mailings

Event	Date
Mailing 1 begins	_____
All material goes to printer	_____
Envelopes stuffed and ready for post office	_____
Mailing delivered to post office	_____
Mailing 2 begins	_____
All material goes to printer	_____
Envelopes stuffed and ready for post office	_____
Mailing delivered to post office	_____

Total cost of acquisition mailings: _____

Special Mailings

Describe your reason for doing a special mailing. It may be a mailing to lapsed donors (people who have not given to your organization for several years), or it may be a special project mailing or a mailing to memorial donors.

Event	Date
All material goes to printer	_____
Envelopes stuffed and ready for post office	_____
Mailing delivered to post office	_____

Total cost of special mailing: _____

All Mailings

Now add up the total cost of all mailings. Include all materials, printing, envelope stuffing, and postal delivery.

Mailing	Total Cost
House List	_____
Acquisition	_____
Special	_____

Total cost of direct mail from _____ (date) to _____ (date): _____

WORKSHEET 6.1 (continued)

Expected Returns

Mailing	Percent Return
House List	_____
Acquisition	_____
Special	_____

Total net income from direct mail: _____

Responsible Persons

It is wise to know ahead of mailing time who will be responsible for certain tasks. Fill in the name of the person or persons responsible for

Mailings

Collecting data

Writing thank-you letters after mailings

Preparing monthly reports after mailings

WORKSHEET 6.2

Budget for an Acquisition Mailing

This worksheet will help you see how to find new friends for your organization. This is a budget for an acquisition mailing—a mailing to people you don't necessarily know. Acquisition mailings are done to bring in new donors and expand the list of supporters. Each year you may lose 25 to 30 percent of your donors, through no fault of your own. People die, move away, or just lose interest in your cause. It is very important that you make new friends for your organization.

Name of Organization: _____

Date of Mailing: _____

Item	Description	Number Needed	Cost
Outer envelope	_____	_____	_____
Postage	_____	_____	_____
Teaser	_____	_____	_____
Letter	_____	_____	_____
Response device	_____	_____	_____
Response device if printed at mailing house	_____	_____	_____
Envelope for response device	_____	_____	_____

Total cost of acquisition mailing: _____

List any other expenses for your mailing, such as a brochure, newspaper clipping, address labels, and so on. Remember, though, that too many items in the mailing may reduce your return.

WORKSHEET 6.3

Estimating Your Mailing Costs

This worksheet will help you make decisions about the mailings you want to send to your house list. You need to know how many donors are on your list and how many times each year you will contact them. I encourage you to contact these donors at least four times per year. Each letter should be carefully crafted to tell a different story regarding the work of your organization and your need for their support.

Let's say you have three thousand names on the house list. This worksheet is set up for one mailing. Therefore, if you mail four times during the year, multiply the three thousand names by four. Thus you will need twelve thousand #10 envelopes, letters, reply devices, and reply envelopes.

Name of Organization: _____

Budget Dates: _____

Item or Service Needed	Number or Frequency	Cost
1. Outer envelope[a]	_____	_____
2. Postage[b]	_____	_____
Use bulk mail indicia? _____		
Use postage meter? _____		
Use mailing house? _____		
3. Teaser	_____	_____
4. Letter	_____	_____
Number of pages _____		
Print in-house? _____		
Print at print shop? _____		
5. Response device[c]	_____	_____
Use business reply envelope? _____		
Use response form from mailing house? _____		

---

[a]Add in extras for special mailings.

[b]First-class postage is 34 cents, so three thousand units would cost $1,020.

[c]If you use a response form from a mailing house, you still need to know the number and cost. Be sure the reply device and a check fit into the reply envelope, which is addressed to your organization. Check the ZIP code if you use a P.O. box.

WORKSHEET 6.3 (continued)

6. Reply envelope[d]   _____   _____

   Type of envelope   _____

   Postage for envelope   _____

7. Other expenses (enclosures)   _____   _____

Total cost of mailing: _____

---

[d]None needed if a BRE is used.

Assessing Your Costs

YOU NOW have your mailing plan for the year. You know the number of mailings, the materials and postage needed, and the cost of any outside help you may need to process these mailings. You have submitted bids to several printers or mailing houses and asked for their prices so you can compare the costs of having the work done. Let's see what a bid might look like.

Printing Costs

To get accurate estimates, you must be very careful to use a form that compares apples to apples. In other words, when asking for a bid, be clear about the number of pieces needed, the weight of the paper, colors to be used, and so on. It is also important to have an agreement with the printer or mailing house regarding the timeline. That is, when will the mailing be ready to go to the post office? Who will deliver the mailing to the post office, and will there be a charge for this delivery? Such decisions result in what are referred to as *production specifications*.

To work through this process, make an outline for each mailing, and get three bids for the production of specific mailings. Printers, mailing houses, list brokers, and mail brokers will be happy to supply you with all of this information in writing. No one will end up being surprised because expenses were not spelled out.

Your budget will be an outline of the funds needed to produce the mailings for one year or whatever time period you are considering in your mailing plan; the total number of envelopes, pieces of stationery, inserts, postage, and other costs must be included. Organizations have specific requirements for their budget presentations. Check with your organization as to their requirements for the presentation of a budget. A very simple budget is shown in Exhibit 7.1.

EXHIBIT 7.1

Sample Printing Budget

Item or Service	Number or Amount	Cost
Envelopes (#10) with logo, return address, and indicia	_____	_____
Letters	_____	_____
Postage:		
First class	_____	_____
Bulk	_____	_____
Bulk annual fee	_____	_____
Printing of business reply envelopes	_____	_____
Printing of response device	_____	_____
Return envelope (if not using BRE)	_____	_____
List broker and list cost	_____	_____
Mail broker, mailing house, or lettershop	_____	_____
Additional costs	_____	_____
	_____	_____
	_____	_____
	_____	_____
Total cost:		_____

In most organizations the yearly direct mail budget will be presented with your annual budget and within your overall fund raising budget. Your annual plan should include the cost of all fund raising activities you plan for a year or for the next eighteen months. This budget might include your mailing cost, cost to reach foundations and corporations, up-front costs for special events, and other ways you plan to raise funds.

The plan should be finished several months before your fiscal or calendar year budget is presented to the board of directors for approval. If you have a history of direct mail fund raising, keep an ongoing account of your expenses and your future budget needs. You should be ready to submit your next-year budget at least four months in advance of the coming fiscal or calendar year. Your coming year's budget will also be affected by your evaluation of the past mailing results. Some mailings may be added or deleted, based on the results of the past year's response.

Tracking Results

Your direct mail efforts must be evaluated as individual efforts; that is, an evaluation must be made of each mailing, followed by an evaluation of the total mailing efforts for a stated period of time (this is discussed in more detail in Chapter Eight). This evaluation will affect your direct mail plans for the coming year and also give you a reliable yardstick against which you can make important decisions.

The evaluation can only be accomplished, however, if you have carefully coded and tracked the income resulting from each mailing. Therefore, the software you use and the management systems you have in place can make or break your evaluation efforts. You will need donor software that allows you to enter codes that define why this gift was received. For each mailing, you'll want to know how many pieces were mailed, the total cost of the mailing, how many gifts were received, the size of the average gift, and the total amount received from the mailing.

From a management standpoint, it is important that all information be entered into the software in a systematic manner. The fund raising director (possibly you) or the direct mail manager must set up a system before the mailings are sent to ensure that you have the information needed for reliable results. If you have several volunteers doing your donor input following a mailing, you will need a written description of how the mailing results are to be entered into the software system. It is very important that all of the volunteers follow the same steps when keying these data to ensure a factual evaluation of the mailing effort.

Once again, a group doing a small mailing (less than five thousand pieces) will have to depend on the response from a specific mailing. That is why it is so important to keep track of the results from each and every mailing that you send. Chapter Eight will give more details on how to do this.

Selecting Donor Software

Select your software carefully. Be wary if well-meaning volunteers offer to build you a software program. Two problems may arise. First, the programs will have no built-in safeguards, and the same names entered in slightly different ways (such as "Mr. and Mrs. Jack Smith" and "Jack and Jane Smith") may end up as separate files. Second, if the person who built your system moves away or is otherwise unavailable, no one else in the office will know how to use, update, or adapt the program.

There are many commercial programs on the market, ranging in cost from $500 to $5,000. Information on fund raising software appears frequently in the *Nonprofit Times* and the *Chronicle of Philanthropy*. Each year, the October issue of *Fund Raising Management* magazine devotes a section to software for nonprofit organizations. The listings give a description of the software, the system specifications, the training or services offered, vendor contact information, and prices.

You can also review donor software by attending the annual conference of the Association of Fundraising Professionals or a local AFP Fund Raising Day in your area. You can also contact organizations in your area and ask what donor software they use and how satisfied they are with it.

If you are just starting to build your donor base, you need not spend a lot of money on a donor software system, but it will be worth its weight in gold in the long run. The system can make it easy for you to keep track of donors, segment your donor base, send thank-you letters, and produce reports. If you think you will be building a very large donor base in the future, you may want to consider a system that can be upgraded as your volume of donor information expands.

When you have reviewed the various systems on the market, contact vendors and ask for the following:

- A booklet describing the software and showing the various screens and reports

- A disk or CD that you can use to view the program

- A list of groups in your area that use the software. (Phone the groups and ask what they think of the program and if they have had any problems.)

You should also phone the vendor's help line several times to find out what kind of service customers can obtain.

Testing and Evaluating Your Direct Mail Efforts

AS I'VE SAID, whether you are mailing to your house list or a cold list, it is wise to test your mailings. If your list is short, testing may not be possible; the returns will be a test in themselves. If your budget permits hiring a direct mail consultant or a list broker, you will be able to do extensive testing.

How to Test

What exactly do I mean by *testing*? Say you have two lists of five hundred names each and want to compare certain variables for results. For example, you may test two different letters—one telling a success story from a program offered by the organization and the other giving information regarding what the organization does and how it helps the clients—to compare the effects of their contents. You can do two mailings using two different letters slanted to two different markets—but realize that *you can test only one variable at a time.* All of the other parts of the package, as described in Chapter Five—outer envelope, letter, enclosures, reply form, and reply envelope— must be identical. You may test just the reply form or just a teaser message versus a picture of a child in need on the outer envelope.

If you are testing a mailing, you must have the ability to measure the results; therefore, all of the mailings must have a source code noting which mailing produced the gift. It is also important to mail the test mailings at the same time or at least within the same week.

Experts claim that you should have five thousand or more names to do a test mailing. Because this book is for organizations that have a very small staff or are run entirely by volunteers, your test may not be as accurate as a large test. But try to glean some insight into which letter or list worked better for your organization. It has been my experience that you can do a test with one thousand names, dividing the list and testing only one variable. This is not as accurate as testing a mailing of five thousand or ten thousand pieces, but it will give some indication of the respondents' reception of your mailing.

Once again, a group doing a small mailing will have to depend on the response from a specific mailing. That is why it is so important to keep track of the results from each and every mailing that you send.

Worksheets

Worksheet 8.1A will help you extract reports from your responses. The filled-in Worksheet 8.1B is provided as a sample.

WORKSHEET 8.1A

How to Evaluate Your Mailings

You have set up the process for evaluation when you coded each return envelope or response form. The results of each mailing have been carefully entered into the donor software system. It is now time to extract reports from the system and analyze the responses from each mailing and the overall mailing for the year or eighteen months. You may wish to use the completed sample (Worksheet 8.1B) as a guide.

Name of Organization: _____

Date of Mailing: _____

Number of pieces: _____

Cost per piece: _____

Total cost of the mailing: _____

Number of replies: _____

Total donations from mailing: _____

Use the data above to calculate percent response, average gift size, net income, and your average cost per gift. These calculations will help you decide whether your fund raising efforts have paid off.

Percent response: This is the number of replies received expressed as a percentage of all who were invited to participate. Divide the number of responses received by the number of solicitations made.

Average gift size: Divide the total contributions received by the number of donors.

Net income: Subtract the full solicitation costs from the total contributions received.

Cost per gift: Divide your fund raising costs by the number of donors.

Using the same formulas, calculate your returns from the acquisition or prospect mailings and any other mailing you have done in the past twelve to eighteen months. Add all of the results to reach a total for all of your mailings.

Now analyze your results from each mailing. Which mailings brought the greatest returns, either in dollars or new donors? Why did one mailing produce more returns than another mailing? This is a subjective evaluation, but the information will be important as you plan the next round of mailings.

WORKSHEET 8.1B

How to Evaluate Your Mailings (Sample)

You may use this worksheet as a guide for filling out Worksheet 8.1A.

Name of Organization: Mid-County Family Shelter

Date of Mailing: April 15, 2001

Number of pieces: 2,225

Cost per piece: $0.30

Total cost of the mailing: $0.30 x 2,225 = $667.50

Number of replies: 610

Total donations from mailing: $5,200

Use the data above to calculate percent response, average gift size, net income, and your average cost per gift. These calculations will help you decide whether your fund raising efforts have paid off.

Percent response: This is the number of replies received expressed as a percentage of all who were invited to participate. Divide the number of responses received by the number of solicitations made.

$$610 \div 2,225 = 27 \text{ percent}$$

Average gift size: Divide the total contributions received by the number of donors.

$$\$5,200 \div 610 = \$8.52$$

Net income: Subtract the full solicitation costs from the total contributions received.

$$\$5,200 - \$667.50 = \$4,532.50$$

Cost per gift: Divide your fund raising costs by the number of donors.

$$\$667.50 \div 610 = \$1.09$$

Using the same formulas, calculate your returns from the acquisition or prospect mailings and any other mailing you have done in the past twelve to eighteen months. Add all of the results to reach a total for all of your mailings.

   Now analyze your results from each mailing. Which mailings brought the greatest returns, either in dollars or new donors? Why did one mailing produce more returns than another mailing? This is a subjective evaluation, but the information will be important as you plan the next round of mailings.

When to Thank

How to Thank

CHAPTER 9

Thanking Your Donors

HOW MANY TIMES should you say thank you to a donor? The thank-you is a very important and necessary part of the direct mail process, and donor recognition is part of the thank-you process. If you cannot send the donor a proper thank-you note within forty-eight hours after receiving the gift, don't bother to start a direct mail program. Your thank-you's let donors know you appreciate their gifts. Treat donors the way you would treat your best friends.

When to Thank

The rule is straightforward: *thank the donor seven times.* The first thank-you is in the letter you send donors asking for support, perhaps in the P.S. It might go something like this: "Your support will make it possible to feed a family of five people for one month. We thank you for your caring." The next is on the return piece or your business reply envelope.

Thank-you number three is sent after you receive the gift. This can be a printed card or a letter that thanks the person for his or her support and includes tax information if necessary. Tax information might include the fact that the gift is over a certain dollar amount and that this acknowledgment should be kept for tax purposes. If a premium has been received and the full amount of the donation is not tax-deductible, the donor must be made aware of that fact as well. Exhibit 9.1 shows a sample thank-you letter for a standard gift; Exhibit 9.2 shows a thank-you letter for a donation of $250 or more.

EXHIBIT 9.1

Sample Thank-You Letter

February 16, 2001

Dear Ms. Jones:

On behalf of the Mid-County Family Shelter, I would like to thank you for your donation of $50, which we received on February 15, 2001.

Thanks to your support, we have been able to help seventy families in the past year. Most of these families have been women with children who needed help putting their lives back together. You have helped provide emergency shelter, food and clothing, jobs for the mothers, and schooling for the children.

With your help, 75 percent of our families are once again productive members of our community.

Thank you once again for your support of others who are having a difficult time.

> Sincerely,
> Michael Edwards
> Volunteer Chair
> Fund Development Committee

EXHIBIT 9.2

Sample Thank-You Letter for a Donation of $250 or More

October 23, 2000

Dear Mr. Graves:

On behalf of Fellowship Hall, Inc., I would like to thank you for your donation of $500.

Your special gift will enable us to complete the work on our new homeless shelter. Once it is completed, the lives of hundreds of people in difficult circumstances will be greatly improved thanks to your generous gift. We thank you from the bottom of our heart.

In accordance with state and federal regulations governing the deductibility of tax-exempt donations to nonprofit organizations, we confirm that no goods or services were received in exchange for this contribution.

> Sincerely,
> Mary Smith
> Program Director
> Fellowship Hall, Inc.

P.S. Please keep this letter for your records and include it when you file your tax return.

How to Thank

Gifts such as T-shirts, mugs, posters, key chains, and bookmarks are low-cost, low-value premiums. If you are considering such giveaways, look into the IRS rules and regulations regarding premiums for charitable donations. These rules change from time to time, and a valuable premium can reduce the donor's contribution deduction, even if the donor receives the premium in a later year.

Part of the thank-you is also recognition—in the organization's newsletter, as part of a donor wall, or at a special event or ceremony. You may want to organize a "thank-you-thon." Have a group of volunteers phone your large donors (after determining what you consider large in your organization) and just thank them for their support and let them know what the organization is doing. In most cases, the donor will be surprised and happy to receive such a call, will feel part of the organization, and will support you once again. This can be a once- or twice-a-year effort, or it can be ongoing. Board members can make a few calls each month to thank donors, find out why they are interested in the organization, and update them on the progress of the programs offered by the organization.

Donors who give smaller gifts may receive a preprinted card that has space to fill in the amount of the gift and space for the date and a signature. It is important that you segment your list and decide who your top donors are. Send them a special letter. You should have on your computer several letters: one for large donors, one for middle-of-the-road donors, one for small donors, and one for special donors such as memorial donors.

I'll say it once more: send a written thank-you within forty-eight hours of receiving the gift. Following that, be creative in the ways you thank and recognize your donors. Thank your donors again and again—at least seven times.

CHAPTER 10

Putting It All Together

IT IS NOW TIME to put your fund raising plans and budget together to be presented to the executive director (if you have one), who will present it to the board of directors for approval. If you are an all-volunteer organization, whoever is in charge of fund raising will present the annual fund raising plan to the board.

Your Annual Budget

Your plan should include all the ways you plan to raise funds during the coming year; it will also include your mailing plans and projected budget. Therefore, about four months before the end of your fiscal or calendar year, your direct mail plan for the coming twelve to eighteen months should be in place and ready to present to the organization. The board of directors must approve the plan and the expenses associated with it. The plan must include your mailing schedule, the budget for mailings, a timeline, and details regarding individual responsibilities for completing each mailing.

Cost guidelines, proposed by several experts in the field of fund development, state that direct mail acquisition will cost $1.25 to $1.50 to raise one dollar. Direct mail renewal—mailings to your house list—will cost $0.20 to $0.25 for each dollar raised. These are general guidelines. It is important that you keep track of your mailings in order to know your cost for each dollar raised. There is no doubt that it will cost you more to bring in new donors than to solicit your present donors. As I've stated several times, it is important that you acquire new donors each year because you lose donors each year. Therefore, your acquisition mailings are an investment in the future. Make friends for the organization.

You have put it all together. Good for you! Once you have followed this process, step by step, for a year or two, you will have a history of returns. Please take the time to follow each step for the first few years of your direct mail program. You will reap outstanding benefits for your organization and become a truly professional fund development executive. Foundations will support you for only a limited time. If you build your donor base through the mail, you will have friends who will support your work over the years.

Resources

Working with the U.S. Postal Service

It is important to go to the post office and talk to the postal workers who handle direct mail. They can be very helpful and will make your mailing a joy, not a trial.

Nonprofit Standard Mail

Qualified nonprofit organizations are eligible to mail at nonprofit standard mail rates, which represent a significant discount from first-class rates. A special permit can be obtained by filing U.S. Postal Service Form 3624, "Application to Mail at Nonprofit Standard Mail Rates."

A responsible officer of your organization must apply for an authorization to mail at the nonprofit standard mail rate at each post office from which mailings will be sent. This authorization requires specific forms and documentation; the application is available at any post office. Your postmaster can answer any questions and help you fill out the form.

The following categories of organization *may* qualify: religious, educational, scientific, philanthropic (charitable), agricultural, labor, veterans, and fraternal. Typical ineligible organizations are chambers of commerce, individuals, service clubs, trade associations, and social and hobby clubs.

It is important that you obtain a copy of the following publications: (1) "Nonprofit Standard Mail Eligibility," Publication No. 417, United States Postal Service, and (2) "Quick Service Guide," Publication No. 95, United States Postal Service. Copies can be obtained at all post offices, business mail entry units, and postal business centers.

The following are the basic requirements for bulk standard mail discount rates, as described in "The Business Guide to Advertising with Direct Mail," published by the U.S. Postal Service:

- All pieces must be in the same category (all letters, all flats, and so on).
- Each mailing must contain at least two hundred addressed pieces or 50 pounds of addressed pieces.
- The correct ZIP code must be on each piece.
- All pieces must qualify as standard mail (no checks, bills, or other material, which must be sent as first-class mail).
- A permit or license to pay postage via nonprofit stamps, permit imprints, or meters must be obtained.
- An annual bulk mailing fee must be paid.

- Mail must be sent from the post office where the permit or license was obtained and the bulk fee paid.
- Mail must be presorted.

Bulk mailing allows you to present large quantities of mail to a particular post office for mailing at lower rates. Several kinds of discounts are available.

Discount for presorting: This means arranging the mail so that pieces going to the same area are bundled together. The more levels of sorting you perform, the lower the cost of postage. Presorted mail must be packaged and labeled in accordance with U.S. Postal Service requirements. Trays, mail sacks, stickers, and labels are available at no charge from your local post office. You should consider your budget, the size of your mailing, and the time sensitivity of your direct mail package. Once again, check the "Quick Service Guide," Publication No. 95.

Discounts for certain designs: Mailers who meet certain mail package design, preparation, and addressing requirements and who apply either delivery point bar codes or ZIP+4 bar codes to their pieces—according to guidelines specified by the Postal Service—receive substantial discounts on their mailings.

Ways to Pay for Bulk Mail

There are three ways to pay for your bulk mail: (1) nonprofit stamps, (2) preprinted indicia (permit imprint), and (3) postage meter.

Nonprofit Stamp or Envelope Permit

Following the completion of Form 3615, "Mailing Permit and Application and Customer Profile," you or your mailing house may affix a nonprofit stamp on each piece of a bulk mailing. This permit is recommended for the lower-volume bulk mailer. Nonprofit stamps may be purchased in lots of five hundred or three thousand at your post office, and the mail pieces must have a domestic return address visible in the upper left-hand corner on the address side. All matter mailed at nonprofit standard mail rates must identify the authorized organization. The authorized organization's name and address must appear in a prominent place on the outside of the mail piece.

Preprinted Indicia or Permit Imprint

Permit imprints also require the completion of Form 3615 and payment of a nonrefundable application fee. You may print or rubber-stamp a permit imprint directly onto the piece in the upper right-corner of the address side.

A permit imprint is a marking containing the permit number, which substitutes for a stamp on each piece of a large mailing. Postage is paid through an account identified by your permit number. Funds may be maintained in the account or deposited before you do a mailing. The permit indicia may not be handwritten or typed. All pieces of the bulk shipment must be identical in weight to allow for verification of the number of pieces by weight.

Postage Meter

Postage meters enable you to pay for large amounts of postage in advance and then use the postage as you need it. Most postage meters today can print in increments of $0.001. This allows you to pay exact presort and bulk mail postage without having to go to the post office. Contact an authorized meter leasing company listed in your business directory under "Mailing Machines" or "Meters."

The leasing company will arrange all of the details, but be sure to inform them you are using bulk mail at nonprofit rates. Permits are obtained at the post office where you intend to mail. After filing the appropriate form, you will receive the authorization to mail. Contact your local post office for application forms and assistance. For additional information and "A Manual of Direct Mail," contact the U.S. Postal Service, P.O. Box 2484, Warminster, PA 18974-0049. This manual will include "The Business Guide to Advertising with Direct Mail."

List Brokers and Mailing Houses

List brokers can help you select lists of individuals who may have some interest in the programs that your organization addresses. The list broker does not own the lists; neither will you own the lists. The lists are leased or rented for one-time use for a specific fee and a specific date, based on the number of names you use. List brokers manage lists for list owners and make a commission on both list rentals and exchanges.

Working with a List Broker

List brokers help direct mailers by doing the following:

- Recommending lists to test

- Helping evaluate tests and selecting lists for roll-outs

- Obtaining approval for list rentals or exchanges (often involves submitting a sample of your letter to the list owner)

- Handling all rental and exchange arrangements

The list broker uses "rate cards" that give you basic information about each list. Not all list brokers service nonprofit organizations, and some list brokers specialize in certain types of nonprofit lists and organizations. To find local list brokers, contact nonprofit organizations similar to your organization, vendors at conferences of the Association of Fundraising Professionals and local Fund Raising Day conferences, the local telephone book, and fund raising magazines, journals, and newspapers.

Some nonprofit organizations trade lists. This practice may upset your board of directors, but experience has shown that donors are not lost due to trading. The trading of lists is quite extensive in the area of the arts and the environment.

The Fund Raising School states that with at least five thousand current donors on your house list, you can trade extensively and significantly reduce the cost of acquisition mailings. With fewer that five thousand names, you can sometimes trade for future use of your list when it grows to five thousand. Another strategy is to trade for multiple uses of your smaller list.

Once you have tested a list with a trade, you can rent the more productive list for the roll-out—the mailing. Some very good lists are only available through trade.

If your organization is worried about donor privacy or the security of your list, your list broker can explain the mechanics and ethics that protect the list owner and the list mailer.

You can also let your donors know that you trade lists and that they can ask that their name not be traded. The Sempervirens Fund in Los Altos, California, an organization for the preservation of redwood land, includes in its newsletter the following statement:

A note to our friends: Occasionally we make our mailing list available on a one-time-only basis to carefully screened organizations with goals similar to those of Sempervirens Fund. If you would prefer that your name not be shared, please drop us a note—we'll be happy to take care of it.

Discuss with the list broker the possibility of duplicate appeals. This can be avoided by merging your list with the lists you are planning to use and thus eliminating any duplicate names. There will be a cost connected with the merge-purge procedure, but in most cases it will save you money on a large mailing. It may also save you many angry phone calls from people who receive multiple solicitations.

Working with a Mailing House

Where do you find a reliable consultant, list broker, or mailing house that has had experience with nonprofit organizations? Is there a nonprofit organization whose offerings you have admired? Call them and find out who works with them to develop their mail. If you are working with a direct mail consultant or a list broker, that person can recommend graphic artists, lettershops, and other support services you may need. Because yours is a nonprofit organization, your budget is tight; get bids, give the process plenty of time, and use your own gut feeling when determining which market you are trying to reach. Will these people react to and respond to your request with a donation? Many professionals can help you find the right list and the right people to put the mailing together and get it to the post office. However, this can be very expensive for small organizations. Up-front efforts put into the mailing will pay dividends in the long run. Find the right people for an organization of your size. You don't need a superstar specialist. You need someone who knows how to get the job done at a reasonable price—a price that fits your budget.

Useful Addresses and Web Sites

The Fund Raising School
Indiana University, Center on Philanthropy
550 West North Street, Suite 301
Indianapolis, IN 46202

Nonprofit Times
240 Cedar Knolls Road, Suite 318
Cedar Knolls, NJ 07927
http://www.nptimes.com

The Chronicle of Philanthropy
P.O. Box 1989
Marion, OH 43306
http://philanthropy.com

Alliance of Nonprofit Mailers
http://www.nonprofitmailers.org

U.S. Postal Service
http://www.usps.com

References

Campbell, B. "Donors Want to Know Where the $$ Goes." *Fund Raising Management Magazine,* July 1998, pp. 40–42.

Craver, R. M. "The Power of Mail to Acquire, Renew, and Upgrade the Gift." In H. A. Rosso and Associates, *Achieving Excellence in Fund Raising: A Comprehensive Guide to Principles, Strategies, and Methods.* San Francisco: Jossey-Bass, 1991.

Grace, K. S. *Beyond Fund Raising.* New York: Wiley, 1997.

Kaplan, A. E. (ed.). *Giving USA 2000.* Indianapolis, Ind.: AAFRC Trust for Philanthropy, 2000.

Keirouz, K., and Rooney, P. "The Philanthropy Giving Index, 1998 Report." [http://www.philanthropy.iupui.edu/pgi-5]. 1998. For updates, consult the Web site or call Kathy Keirouz at (317) 684-8957.

Rosso, H. A. "The Annual Fund: A Building Block for Fund Raising." In H. A. Rosso and Associates, *Achieving Excellence in Fund Raising: A Comprehensive Guide to Principles, Strategies, and Methods.* San Francisco: Jossey-Bass, 1991a.

Rosso, H. A. "Preparing a Case That Empowers Fund Raising." In H. A. Rosso and Associates, *Achieving Excellence in Fund Raising: A Comprehensive Guide to Principles, Strategies, and Methods.* San Francisco: Jossey-Bass, 1991b.

Rosso, H. A. "Understanding the Fund Raising Cycle." In H. A. Rosso and Associates, *Achieving Excellence in Fund Raising: A Comprehensive Guide to Principles, Strategies, and Methods.* San Francisco: Jossey-Bass, 1991c.

Warwick, M. *Revolution in the Mailbox.* Berkeley, Calif.: Strathmoor Press, 1990.

Further Reading

Help Writing Letters

Cone, A. L., Jr. *How to Create and Use Solid Gold Fund-Raising Letters.* Rockville, Md.: Fund Raising Institute, Taft Group, 1987.

Huntsinger, J. *Fundraising Letters.* (2nd ed.) Richmond, Va.: Emerson, 1985.

Kuniholm, R. *The Complete Book of Model Fund-Raising Letters.* Paramus, N.J.: Prentice Hall, 1995.

Lewis, H. G. *How to Write Powerful Fund Raising Letters.* Chicago: Bonus Books, 1989.

Warwick, M. *How to Write Successful Fundraising Letters.* San Francisco: Jossey-Bass, 2001.

Warwick, M. *How to Write Successful Fundraising Letters.* Berkeley, Calif.: Strathmoor Press, 1994.

Fund Raising Help

Greenfield, J. M. *Fund Raising Cost Effectiveness: A Self-Assessment Workbook.* New York: Wiley, 1996.

Hamilton, G. *Fundraiser's Phrase Book.* Toronto, Canada: Hamilton House, 1996.

Klein, K. *Fundraising for Social Change: Grassroots Fundraising Journal.* Berkeley, Calif.: Chardon Press, 1994.

Lautman, K. P., and Goldstein, H. *Dear Friend: Mastering the Art of Direct Mail Fund Raising.* Washington, D.C.: Taft Group, 1984.

Seymour, H. J. *Designs for Fund-Raising.* (2nd ed.) Ambler, Pa.: Fund-Raising Institute, 1988.

9 780787 955298